REST ASSURED

Conquering Insomnia, And Unlocking the Path To Peaceful Sleep

By

Bradley R. Edmonds

Being unable to sleep is a regular occurrence. In reality, studies show that about a third of adults suffer from chronic insomnia, a sleep disease marked by ongoing problems sleeping or staying asleep.

National Library of Medicine,
Biotech Information

Sleep problems are frequently caused by anxiety and stress. The body's natural stress reaction kicks in during times of tension, starting with a cascade of chemicals that increase our alertness and cause subsequent physiological changes.

American Psychological Association (APA)

Who is this book for, then?
This book is for anyone who has trouble falling or staying asleep, or who suffers from insomnia.
anyone taking sleep medicine who is apprehensive, stressed, or worried about their sleep.
If you want to permanently eradicate insomnia and fall asleep faster, sleep deeper, and wake up relaxed and with energy, then this book is for you. It is for anyone who is feeling exhausted, fatigued, or in a bad mood during the day.

So this is what this book will be talking about: how to get rid of insomnia for good without using any external cures or medications.

how to consistently achieve deep, healthy-quality sleep over time, even if your current sleep is disturbed, stressful, and unpredictable.

No matter how long you've had trouble sleeping, there are ways to fall asleep more quickly, sleep longer, and wake up feeling refreshed and restored.

How to transform from being wired and awake in bed to being peaceful and drowsy even if this seems impossible right now How to get rid of anxiety, worry, and tension over your sleep and develop perfect confidence that you can and will sleep well every night

No matter how long you've felt this way, here's how to stop feeling sleepy, fatigued, and exhausted during the day while also having a fuzzy head.

even if you think you've lost the skill, learn how to uplift your mood and perform better in your career and personal life.

This book will teach you effective, scientifically-based sleep-improvement practices and will walk you through a step-by-step plan for putting an end to insomnia once and for all. But before we get to the good stuff, let me briefly check in with you to see how you're doing.

Does this describe you?

Do you secretly dread going to bed because you're worried it'll be another night of tension, worry, irritation, and a struggle to get any rest?

Do you toss and turn in bed at night, wired or aware, while everyone else in the room is fast asleep?

Have you tried sleeping aids, drugs, supplements, herbs, or other things but discovered they didn't work very well or at all and had terrible side effects?

Do you worry about how insomnia and insufficient sleep may affect your overall health, happiness, sanity, and well-being in the long run?

Do you fear that if you don't get enough sleep, you won't be able to perform effectively at work or be a decent parent the next day?

Do you worry that you can no longer fall asleep or stay asleep, that something is seriously wrong with your body, possibly something that cannot be fixed?

Do you feel like you've tried everything to get better sleep, and you're frightened, disheartened, and hopeless that this will ever change? I have good news if any of that applies to you. Get rid of your insomnia for good by purchasing **REST ASSURED** today.

Dear reader(s),

As you begin on this groundbreaking excursion towards peaceful sleep, I believe you should realize that you are in good company. The way you are struggling has been gone through by a larger number of people before you, each moving toward a similar objective, nights of serene sleep and mornings of restored energy. I praise you for making this stride and for deciding to focus on your prosperity and recover the quietness that rest can bring. Keep in mind, the difficulties you face are not unconquerable; they are the venturing stones that will lead you to a position of solace and calm.

All through these pages, you will find an embroidery of methods, insight, and stories woven to direct you. You grasp the apparatuses to reassure you, relieve your soul, and embrace the delicate hug of rest. The excursion might have its exciting bends in the road, however with each step in the right direction, you are drawing nearer to your objective.

There might be minutes when progress appears to be slow and the evenings are as yet anxious. In those times, recollect that change takes time, and every work you make, regardless of how little, is a positive development. Show restraint toward yourself and trust the cycle. You are equipped for change of breaking, liberated from the grasp of restless evenings. As you dig into these pages, permit yourself to embrace the potential outcomes that lie ahead. Envision the mornings loaded up with energy, the days set apart by clearness, and the nights enveloped by the cover of tranquil dreams. Realize that each work you set forth and each procedure you practice carries you nearer to the relaxing rest you merit. Also, as you venture as the night progresses, consistently recall that you are more grounded than any sleep challenge, and more splendid mornings look for you not too far off.

Rest well, dream openly, and may your nights be loaded up with the commitment of calm.

With warmth and support,

Bradley

Disclaimer

The information provided in this book is intended for general guidance and educational purposes only. It is not a substitute for professional medical advice, diagnosis, or treatment. Readers should consult with a qualified healthcare provider before making any changes to their sleep habits or lifestyle. The author and publisher are not liable for any actions taken based on the information presented in this book

Table of contents

Introduction

A voyage into the world of sound sleep awaits in the stillness of the hours before dawn when the rest of the world sleeps. A setting where tensions and worries evaporate and the mind finds comfort in the calming embrace of dreams. Welcome to a transforming journey created by the whisper of the night and geared toward anyone looking to tame their nighttime agitation and find the key to calm slumber. Sleep is frequently an elusive friend in today's fast-paced world when demands and diversions jumble with our thoughts. The enigmatic insomnia steals the peace we long for by lurking in the shadows of our nights. But do not worry; you will find a tapestry of knowledge and methods weaved to enlighten the route in these pages.

This is more than simply a book; it is a path to renewal and a voyage of self-discovery. Discover the science of sleep, the art of relaxation, and the control of stress as you read the pages that follow. You will explore the mental landscapes while learning how to calm the turbulent thought currents that prevent you from falling asleep.

You will set out on a transforming journey, guided by the wisdom of sleep specialists, mindfulness practitioners, and individuals who have triumphed over their sleep challenges. You'll discover how to quiet the din of worry, welcome the stillness of the night, and rediscover the restorative embrace of sound sleep. Are you prepared to change the way your nights are described? to say goodbye to restless wanderings and welcome the promise of each fresh dawn? Let's go out on this expedition together, and may our journey take us to the serene shores of restorative sleep. **Turn the page because the journey is about to begin, but before, calculate how much your sleeplessness is costing you.** Your physical health, emotional health, relationships, and general quality of life can all suffer as a result of insomnia, which can also hurt other areas of your life. A compromised immune system, cardiovascular disorders, obesity, diabetes, and other health problems are all linked to insomnia at an elevated risk. Over time, these disorders may be exacerbated by persistent sleep deprivation. A lot of times, mood disorders like anxiety and depression, and insomnia go hand in hand. These disorders can worsen if you don't get enough sleep, creating a vicious cycle where lack of sleep causes mental health to deteriorate and vice versa.

Cognitive processes like memory, attention, concentration, and decision-making can be impacted by sleep deprivation. It may result in lower productivity, attention issues, and a decreased capacity for problem-solving.

You may become more emotionally sensitive and prone to mood swings if you have sleep problems. When sleep is disturbed, irritability, impatience, and heightened emotional responses are frequently experienced.

Reduced performance at work or in the classroom may result from insomnia. It can become difficult to focus on work, process information, and finish assignments.

Lack of sleep can make a person irritable and emotionally unstable, which could put a strain on relationships with friends, family, and coworkers.

The severe daytime sleepiness and weariness that insomnia frequently causes make normal activities like driving, working, and even socializing more challenging and sometimes dangerous. Your capacity for engaging in fun activities, pursuing hobbies, and maintaining a fulfilling social life can all be negatively impacted by insomnia, which can have a substantial effect on your overall quality of life.

Chronic sleep loss can raise the risk of accidents in the workplace, diminish work performance, and cause absenteeism. Due to a lack of restorative sleep, insomnia can make it more difficult for the body to deal with stressors, which can increase stress levels.

compromised immune system Immune system health is critically important. Due to a weakened immune system caused by insomnia, you are more likely to contract diseases and infections. Chronic sleep problems have been associated with early skin aging, which results in wrinkles, fine lines, and a dull complexion.

It's critical to understand that treating insomnia and enhancing sleep can have significant positive consequences, potentially reversing or reducing many of these expenditures. Let's check out what is installed for you now.

How to use this book

This book is subdivided into seven (7) chapters, starting from chapter one which talks about understanding insomnia, the types of insomnia, symptoms, causes, and even the consequences of insomnia to you.

Chapter two explains sleep fundamentals, the different stages of sleep, and the importance of a good night's sleep.

Chapter three explains the symptoms of insomnia including addressing the cause of sleeplessness, having good sleep hygiene, how important it is, and why you should maintain it.

Chapter four talks about sleep logs, their importance, and why you should keep one.

Chapter five explains the five steps to addressing insomnia and getting rid of it forever

Chapter six this is where you learn how to prevent relapse and then the conclusion.

Chapter One

UNDERSTANDING INSOMNIA

A frequent sleep problem known as insomnia is characterized by challenges with falling asleep, remaining asleep, or having unrefreshing sleep while having the chance to do so. People who suffer from insomnia frequently struggle to obtain enough sleep or to sleep soundly or deeply, which can have a variety of detrimental implications on their physical and mental health.

The two main categories of insomnia are:

Primary Insomnia: This kind of insomnia is not brought on by a different illness or outside cause. It frequently has something to do with things like stress, worry, sadness, or bad sleeping habits.

Secondary Insomnia: In this situation, sleeplessness is a sign of a more serious medical issue, such as persistent pain, asthma, or specific neurological diseases. It may also be an adverse reaction to drugs, beverages like coffee or alcohol, or disturbances in the sleep environment (such as light or noise).

types of insomnia according to length

Acute Insomnia: Acute insomnia is a temporary sleep disorder that normally lasts a few days to a few weeks. It is frequently brought on by particular occurrences or circumstances in life, such as stress, jet lag, schedule disruptions, illness, or environmental causes. A few lifestyle changes or addressing the underlying reason can generally make acute insomnia bearable. Sleep patterns usually return to normal after the triggering occasion or circumstance has passed. Acute insomnia is a common problem that many people encounter at some time in their lives.

Chronic Insomnia: On the other hand, chronic insomnia is a long-term sleep disturbance that lasts for three months or longer. Contrary to acute insomnia, persistent insomnia is not always linked to a specific triggering event and frequently has more complicated root causes. It may be a result of underlying illnesses, psychological disorders, or recurring behaviors that disturb sleep.

Chronic insomnia can have a substantial negative effect on a person's quality of life, as it can damage their mood, cognitive ability, productivity at work, and general health. Due to diminished attentiveness, it can cause daytime weariness, irritation, difficulties concentrating, and an elevated risk of accidents.

Chronic insomnia has a variety of causes, including:

Psychological Factors: Consistent sleep problems may be exacerbated by long-term stress, anxiety, depression, and other mental health illnesses.

Medical Conditions: Sleep disturbances can be caused by neurological illnesses, respiratory issues, digestive issues, and chronic pain conditions.

Substance Abuse: Prolonged use of drugs, alcohol, caffeine, nicotine, or nicotine-containing products can interfere with sleep cycles.

Poor Sleep Habits: Chronic insomnia can be sustained by persistently inconsistent sleep habits, excessive naps, or participating in stimulating activities before bed.

Sleep Environment: Discomfortable sleeping conditions, loud noises, or high or low temperatures in the bedroom can make it difficult to get to sleep and stay asleep.

There are several ways that insomnia might appear, including:

Having trouble falling asleep: Takes a while to nod off once in bed.

Awakening frequently throughout the night and having problems settling back to sleep.

Unable to fall back asleep after being awakened before the required or desired amount of sleep has been obtained.

Non-restorative sleep: Feeling exhausted and unrefreshed despite having slept for a sufficient length of time.

A person's general health may be significantly impacted by chronic insomnia, which can also increase their chance of developing mood disorders (such as depression and anxiety), decrease their cognitive ability, diminish their productivity, and increase their risk of accidents because of daytime sleepiness.

Insomnia symptoms include:
- difficulty sleeping at night
- frequent nighttime awakenings
- early morning awakening and inability to fall back asleep
- feeling exhausted when you wake up
- Daytime drowsiness or weariness
- irritability, emotional instability, or difficulty focusing
- reduced performance in work or school as a result of sleep deprivation

Causes of insomnia

Insomnia can have several reasons, some of which include:

High levels of stress or chronic concern might make it difficult to unwind and go to sleep.

Poor Sleep Habits: The natural sleep-wake cycle can be thrown off by irregular sleep schedules, excessive naps, or participating in stimulating activities right before bed.

Depression, anxiety disorders, and post-traumatic stress disorder (PTSD) are examples of mental health conditions that can cause sleeplessness.

Medical Conditions: Sleep disturbances can be caused by chronic pain, respiratory issues, neurological conditions, and hormone imbalances.

Medication: Several drugs, including stimulants, antidepressants, and asthma or allergy treatments, may interfere with sleep.

Alcohol, nicotine, caffeine, and recreational substances can all have an impact on how well you sleep.

Ambient factors that affect sleep quality include uncomfortable bedding, excessive noise, and sweltering temperatures in the bedroom.

The typical course of treatment for insomnia entails addressing the underlying causes and establishing good sleep hygiene habits, such as maintaining regular sleep schedules, creating a comfortable sleeping environment, limiting stimulants (such as caffeine and nicotine) close to bedtime, managing stress, and occasionally, if necessary, recommending behavioral therapy or medications. Let's continue.

Cognitive behavioral therapy for insomnia (CBT-I) is a very successful, evidence-based treatment strategy that aids people in recognizing and altering unfavorable cognitive patterns and sleep-related behaviors.

Establishing sound sleep practices, such as adhering to a regular sleep schedule, developing a calming nighttime routine, and improving the sleep environment.

Medication: Short-term sleep drugs are often prescribed by doctors to help patients break the cycle of insomnia, but they should normally be used with caution due to the possibility of dependence and negative effects.

Addressing the Root Causes: Treating any medical or psychological issues that cause insomnia will help you sleep better.

Meditation, deep breathing exercises, progressive muscle relaxation, and other relaxation methods can all be used to assist the body and mind to rest before bed.

numerous detrimental impacts on one's physical and mental health

Numerous detrimental impacts of insomnia can be seen on both physical and mental health. The following are some of the most typical effects of prolonged sleep loss brought on by insomnia:

Physical Consequences

Daytime weariness: Consistent sleep deprivation causes daytime sleepiness and weariness, which make it difficult for a person to focus and carry out everyday chores efficiently.

Immune system weakness: Sleep is essential for immune function, and long-term insomnia can compromise immunity, leaving people more prone to infections and illnesses.

Increased Risk of Chronic Health Issues: Heart disease, diabetes, obesity, and hypertension have all been related to an increased risk of chronic health issues among long-term insomnia patients.

Impairment of Cognitive Function: Sleep is essential for cognitive activities like learning, problem-solving, and memory consolidation. In several places, insomnia might cause problems.

Reduced Physical Coordination: Lack of sleep can have a bad effect on one's ability to move and coordinate their body, which raises the possibility of accidents and injuries.

Weight Gain: Lack of sleep can throw off the hormones that control hunger, causing an increase in appetite and a higher chance of gaining weight.

Lack of sleep can lower the pain threshold and increase sensitivity to pain, aggravating diseases associated with chronic pain.

Effects on the mind and emotions:

Mood Disorders: Depression and anxiety are two mood disorders that are closely related to insomnia. Lack of sleep can exacerbate current mood problems and lead to the emergence of new ones.

Irritability and Emotional Instability: People who lack sleep are more likely to be irritable, moody, and emotionally unstable.

Lack of sleep can affect cognitive processes, particularly judgment, and decision-making, which can result in erroneous decisions and poor judgment.

Insomnia can impair a person's capacity to deal with stress healthily, making it more difficult to control daily stressors.

Reduced Quality of Life: Chronic insomnia can have a considerable negative influence on a person's overall quality of life, which can cause them to feel less satisfied with their jobs, their relationships, and their leisure time.

Mental Health diseases: Severe and untreated insomnia may exacerbate or cause the onset of mental health diseases, such as anxiety disorders, mood disorders, and in certain circumstances, psychotic symptoms.

Potential causes of insomnia

Numerous variables may contribute to insomnia, and it frequently has multiple possible causes. To properly treat and manage the illness, it is crucial to identify the underlying reasons for insomnia. Here are a few typical probable insomnia causes:

Stress and anxiety: Upsetting life events, pressures at work, concerns about money, or major life changes can cause heightened anxiety, which makes it difficult to unwind and go to sleep.

Psychological Disorders: Sleep patterns can be disturbed by conditions including depression, generalized anxiety disorder, post-traumatic stress disorder (PTSD), and other mental health problems.

Poor Sleep Habits: Poor sleep habits include irregular sleep schedules, inconsistent nighttime routines, excessive daytime naps, and utilizing electronic gadgets right before bed.

Stimulants: Consuming caffeine or other stimulants (such as cigarettes) right before bed might make it difficult to get to sleep and stay asleep.

Medication: Insomnia may be a side effect of various drugs, including some antidepressants, asthma treatments, decongestants, and stimulants.

Chronic pain ailments, respiratory conditions including asthma or sleep apnea, digestive problems, and neurological disorders can all interfere with sleep.

Alcohol, recreational drugs, and some prescriptions taken incorrectly can all cause sleep problems due to substance abuse.

Environmental Factors: Discomfortable sleeping conditions and environmental factors including noise, light, and temperature can all cause insomnia.

Hormonal Changes: Hormone fluctuations can have an impact on sleep patterns, notably in women during menstrual cycles, pregnancy, or menopause.

Age: Older persons are more likely to experience insomnia, perhaps as a result of altered sleep habits and aging-related medical disorders.

Rapid time zone changes or erratic work schedules can throw off the body's natural circadian cycle, making it harder to fall asleep.

RLS: A condition that causes the impulse to move your legs and is frequently accompanied by unpleasant feelings. Falling asleep can be difficult with RLS.

Fear or anxiety over being unable to fall asleep might start a cycle of sleeplessness that eventually results in insomnia.

Excessive Worry: It can be difficult to relax and go to sleep when you are worrying excessively, especially before night.

Other sleep disorders, such as sleep apnea, narcolepsy, and periodic limb movement disorder, can interfere with sleep and cause insomnia in addition to the condition itself.

It's crucial to keep in mind that some people might experience a combination of these causes, and the underlying causes could alter over time. The core reasons for insomnia may be found and addressed through self-help techniques, dietary adjustments, stress reduction techniques, and, in certain situations, professional advice or medical care. To diagnose insomnia and create an effective treatment plan, it can be helpful to speak with a healthcare professional or a sleep expert.

Chapter two

Sleep fundamental

Understanding and recognizing the importance of sleep, having a consistent sleep schedule, and adopting appropriate sleep hygiene habits are critical for fostering optimal health and well-being.

The sleep-wake cycle is a key element of human physiology and plays a crucial role in sustaining overall health and well-being. Sleep is a naturally recurring state characterized by altered consciousness and diminished sensory activity, during which the body conducts several restorative processes. Several fundamental features of sleep include:

Circadian Rhythm: The sleep-wake cycle is regulated by the circadian rhythm, an internal biological clock that roughly follows a 24-hour pattern. It regulates the timing of when we feel alert and when we feel tired. The circadian rhythm is primarily controlled by environmental cues, such as light and darkness, and serves to synchronize the body's sleep-wake rhythms with the day-night cycle.

Sleep Architecture: Sleep comprises of various stages that repeat in cycles throughout the night. These stages include non-REM (rapid eye movement) sleep and REM sleep. Non-REM sleep is further separated into three stages (N1, N2, N3) signifying increasingly deeper sleep. REM sleep is the stage where vivid dreaming occurs, and the brain activity is similar to that of being awake.

Sleep Homeostasis: The body has a built-in sleep homeostatic mechanism that manages the balance between sleep and awake. The longer someone stays up, the stronger the drive to sleep grows. Sleep debt, acquired through insufficient sleep over time, might alter the intensity and duration of subsequent sleep cycles.

Neurotransmitters and Hormones: The sleep-wake cycle is regulated by several neurotransmitters and hormones in the brain. Melatonin, frequently referred to as the "sleep hormone," helps regulate sleep onset and is controlled by the circadian cycle. Adenosine is a neurotransmitter that builds up during alertness and contributes to the feeling of tiredness.

Restoration and Repair: Sleep plays a critical function in bodily and mental restoration. During sleep, the body heals tissues, consolidates memories, and increases learning processes. Sleep is also necessary for immunological function and hormone balance.

Necessity for Health: Adequate sleep is crucial for preserving physical health, cognitive function, emotional well-being, and overall performance. Chronic sleep deprivation or interruptions can lead to a range of health problems and significantly influence the quality of life.

Individual Variation: Sleep demands might differ among individuals. While most individuals require 7-9 hours of sleep per night, some people may function effectively with slightly less or slightly more sleep. Sleep demands may also fluctuate with age and lifestyle circumstances.

Sleep Disorders: Various sleep disorders can disrupt the normal sleep-wake cycle, including insomnia, sleep apnea, narcolepsy, restless legs syndrome, and others. Identifying and treating these issues is vital for maintaining healthy sleep patterns.

Stages of sleep fundamental.

Throughout the night, the sleep cycle repeats, with each cycle lasting roughly 90-110 minutes. The proportion of time spent in each sleep stage fluctuates throughout the night, with more time devoted to deep N3 sleep in the early part of the night and more time spent in REM sleep during the later half of the night. Sleep consists of various stages that repeat in cycles throughout the night. These stages are typically divided into two basic types: non-rapid eye movement (non-REM) sleep and rapid eye movement (REM) sleep. Each stage has distinct properties and serves different purposes in the sleep-wake cycle. Here's an overview of the stages of sleep:

Non-Rapid Eye Movement (non-REM) Sleep:
Non-REM sleep is the initial phase of sleep and is further separated into three stages: N1, N2, and N3. As the sleep cycle unfolds, the phases become progressively deeper, with N3 being the deepest state of sleep. The body spends a large chunk of the night in non-REM sleep.

Stage N1 (NREM 1):

Light sleep stage.

The transition between wakefulness and sleep. Muscle activity reduces, and eye movements are slow. Hypnic jerks (sudden muscular contractions) may occur. People in this stage can be readily aroused. Lasts for a few minutes.

Stage N2 (NREM 2):

Deeper sleep stage.

Eye movements stop, and brain waves become slower with intermittent bursts of fast brain activity.

Sleep spindles (short bursts of brain activity) and K-complexes (sudden high-amplitude waves) may occur.

Body temperature lowers, and heart rate slows down.

Accounts for a considerable chunk of total sleep time.

Stage N3 (NREM 3):

The deep sleep stage is also known as slow-wave sleep (SWS).

Characterized by sluggish brain waves (delta waves).

It is tough to wake someone in this stage.

Growth hormone is secreted at this stage, encouraging physical restoration and repair.

Important for total physical recovery and restorative processes.

Rapid Eye Movement (REM) Sleep:
REM sleep is the stage linked with intense dreaming and enhanced brain activity, resembling alertness in many ways. It happens roughly 90 minutes after falling asleep and recurs numerous times during the night, often getting longer in the later cycles.

REM (Rapid Eye Movement):
Brain activity increases, resembling awake.
Rapid and erratic eye movements.
Muscles are briefly immobilized (sleep paralysis) to prevent acting out dreams.
Most dreaming happens during REM sleep.
Important for cognitive activities like memory consolidation and emotional processing.
Supports learning and brain plasticity.

Recognizing the importance of a good night's sleep
Understanding the different sleep stages might help you grasp the importance of having a good night's sleep for general health and well-being. By knowing how each sleep stage contributes to many elements of health and functioning, you can realize the necessity of prioritizing sleep and maintaining healthy sleep patterns. A consistent and restorative

sleep schedule is vital for general physical health, mental well-being, and overall quality of life.

Here's how each sleep stage contributes to this understanding:

Stage N1 (NREM 1): This is the initial stage of sleep when we move from wakefulness to sleep. It is a light slumber stage where people can be readily roused. If someone has difficulties falling asleep or spends too much time in this stage owing to different factors like stress or poor sleep patterns, they may not obtain enough restorative sleep during the night.

Stage N2 (NREM 2): Deeper than N1, this stage is marked by sleep spindles and K-complexes. N2 sleep is crucial for memory consolidation and learning. If someone's sleep is interrupted or they don't spend enough time in this stage, it can impact their cognitive skills and memory recall.

Stage N3 (NREM 3): This is the deep sleep stage or slow-wave sleep (SWS) where delta waves dominate brain activity. It is vital for physical restoration, growth hormone release, and total bodily repair. A lack of appropriate time spent in this stage may contribute to increased feelings of exhaustion and poor physical recovery.

REM (Rapid Eye Movement) Sleep: This is the period where vivid dreaming happens.
Emotional processing and memory consolidation are linked to REM sleep. REM sleep disruptions can result in emotional issues, trouble managing mood, and impaired cognitive performance.

By comprehending the relevance of each sleep stage, readers can realize the following crucial points:
Quality of Sleep: Getting a good night's sleep includes cycling through all sleep stages many times in a balanced manner. A disturbance in any stage or skipping specific stages can lead to sleep loss and impact the overall restorative activities of sleep.
Physical Health: Deep N3 sleep is vital for physical recovery and repair, as growth hormone is released during this period. Lack of deep sleep can impair immunological function, promote inflammation, and elevate the chance of developing chronic health disorders.

Cognitive Functioning: Both NREM and REM sleep stages are crucial for cognitive processes, memory consolidation, and learning. Adequate sleep enables excellent cognitive performance, problem-solving ability, and creativity.

Emotional Well-being: REM sleep, with its involvement in emotional processing and regulation, is crucial for emotional well-being and mental health. Disruptions in REM sleep can lead to emotional instability and may contribute to mood disorders.

Overall Performance: A good night's sleep significantly improves alertness, focus, and productivity during the day. Sleep-deprived persons are more prone to impaired performance and a higher risk of accidents.

The circadian rhythm is a natural, endogenous process that regulates the sleep-wake cycle and repeats roughly every 24 hours. It is also known as the body's inherent biological clock. This rhythm is influenced by environmental cues such as light and darkness and is crucial in determining when we are awake and conscious and when we are asleep

Key components of the circadian rhythm include:

Suprachiasmatic Nucleus (SCN): The circadian rhythm is principally controlled by a group of cells in the brain called the suprachiasmatic nucleus (SCN). It is positioned in the hypothalamus and operates as the master clock that synchronizes different physiological processes with the day-night cycle.

Light-Dark Cycle: The key external trigger that regulates the circadian rhythm is exposure to light. When the retina of our eyes senses light, it sends messages to the SCN, signifying that it is daytime. In reaction, the SCN reduces the production of the sleep hormone melatonin, encouraging wakefulness. In the absence of light, such as during the evening and midnight, the SCN permits melatonin production to increase, promoting sleepiness.

Sleep-Wake Patterns: The circadian rhythm regulates the time of our sleep-wake patterns. Most people experience a natural fall in alertness and a desire to sleep during the late evening and early morning hours, whereas they are normally most aware during the afternoon.

Disruptions to the circadian rhythm, also known as circadian misalignment, can arise due to many circumstances, such as:

- Shift Work
- Jet Lag
- Irregular Sleep Schedule

- Exposure to Artificial Light at Night
- Travel and Time Zone Changes

When the circadian rhythm is interrupted, it can contribute to insomnia by causing the following:

Difficulty Falling Asleep: Circadian misalignment can delay the onset of sleep, making it challenging to fall asleep at the intended bedtime.

Sleep Fragmentation: The circadian rhythm determines the architecture of sleep, including the timing and duration of each sleep stage. Disruptions to this pattern can lead to fragmented sleep and poor sleep efficiency.

Early Morning Awakening: Circadian disruptions may lead to early morning awakenings before the required quantity of sleep is reached.

Reduced Sleep Quality: Insomnia induced by circadian abnormalities can result in less restorative sleep, leading to daytime sleepiness, weariness, and reduced daily functioning

Chapter Three

Common insomnia triggers

Insomnia can be induced by different factors, and understanding these triggers is vital for managing and increasing sleep quality. Identifying and resolving these insomnia triggers can greatly improve sleep quality. Practicing excellent sleep hygiene, maintaining a regular sleep schedule, reducing stress, and creating a comfortable sleep environment are crucial elements in managing insomnia and encouraging restful sleep.

Common insomnia triggers include:

Stress and Anxiety: Experiencing high levels of stress or chronic anxiety can contribute to trouble falling asleep or staying asleep. Racing thoughts and worries may keep the mind active at night, making it tough to relax and initiate sleep. Here's how stress and worry can interrupt sleep considerably more and contribute to insomnia:

Hyperarousal: When a person feels stress or worry, the body's natural stress response is stimulated, resulting in greater physiological arousal. This hyperarousal condition might make it difficult for the body to relax and transition into sleep.

Racing Thoughts: Stress and anxiety can result in racing thoughts and excessive worrying, especially during nighttime when there are fewer distractions. The mind becomes absorbed with issues, making it tough to calm the thoughts and fall into slumber.

Delayed Sleep Onset: Stress and worry can delay the onset of sleep, as individuals may spend longer time lying in bed, trying to sleep but unable to do so. This can lead to frustration and further exacerbate sleep troubles.

Nighttime Awakenings: Stress and worry can contribute to repeated awakenings during the night. Individuals may wake up feeling aware and unable to return to sleep owing to ongoing worry or unwanted thoughts.

Fragmented Sleep: The heightened arousal and frequent awakenings can lead to fragmented sleep, where individuals have multiple brief awakenings throughout the night. This results in diminished sleep continuity and less restorative sleep.

Cortisol Levels: Stress triggers the release of cortisol, the stress hormone. Elevated cortisol levels at night can interfere with the natural drop in cortisol, which typically happens in the evening to promote relaxation and sleep.

bodily Symptoms: Stress and anxiety can also appear in bodily symptoms such as muscle tightness, headaches, and gastrointestinal pain, which can be disruptive to sleep.

The cycle of Worry and Sleeplessness: The fear of not getting enough sleep or the concern about the repercussions of insomnia can generate a cycle of worry. This fear, in turn, reinforces insomnia, as the anticipation of sleep difficulties can lead to increased tension and anxiety at bedtime.

Poor Sleep Habits: Irregular sleep schedules, irregular bedtime practices, and participating in stimulating activities close to bedtime can disturb the body's natural sleep-wake cycle.

Caffeine and Stimulants: Consuming caffeine (found in coffee, tea, energy drinks, and some pharmaceuticals) or other stimulants late in the day can interfere with the ability to fall asleep.

Electronic gadgets: The blue light emitted by electronic gadgets (e.g., cellphones, tablets, computers) might block the production of melatonin, the sleep hormone, making it difficult to fall asleep.

Environmental Factors: unpleasant sleep circumstances, such as excessive noise, light, or an unpleasant mattress, might impair falling asleep or staying asleep.

Medical Conditions: Chronic pain, respiratory illnesses like asthma or sleep apnea, gastrointestinal troubles, and neurological disorders all cause discomfort and impair sleep.

drugs: Certain drugs, including some antidepressants, asthma treatments, decongestants, and stimulants, may have sleeplessness as a side effect.

Alcohol and Substance Use: Alcohol and recreational drugs can significantly affect sleep quality and interrupt the sleep cycle.

Jet Lag and Shift Work: Rapid time zone changes or irregular work patterns can disturb the body's intrinsic circadian cycle, leading to sleep issues.

Hormonal Changes: Hormonal shifts during the menstrual cycle, pregnancy, or menopause might impact sleep patterns in women.

Food and Eating Habits: Consuming big meals, spicy or acidic foods, or drinking excessive fluids before night can lead to discomfort and impair sleep.

Travel & Time Zone Changes: Traveling to different time zones can create jet lag, leading to temporary sleep problems.

Age: Insomnia becomes more common with age, generally due to changes in sleep habits and age-related health issues.

Psychological Disorders: Conditions such as depression, generalized anxiety disorder, post-traumatic stress disorder (PTSD), and other mental health concerns can affect sleep patterns.

Sleep Anxiety or Fear of Insomnia: Fear or anxiety about not being able to sleep can establish a cycle of sleeplessness, leading to insomnia.

Addressing the causes of sleeplessness
1. Sleep hygiene

A bedroom environment and daily habits that promote regular, undisturbed sleep are essential components of good sleep hygiene. Excellent sleep hygiene can be achieved by maintaining a regular sleep schedule, keeping your bedroom relaxing and distraction-free, engaging in a calming pre-bed ritual, and forming healthy daily routines.

Everybody can adjust their sleep hygiene routines to meet their needs. In the process, you can set beneficial behaviors to make it simpler to sleep peacefully throughout the night and wake up fully anew.

Why Is Sleep Hygiene Important?

Obtaining proper sleep is vital for both physical and mental health, enhancing productivity and general quality of life. Everyone, from children to elderly adults, can benefit from better sleep, and sleep hygiene can play a crucial part in attaining that objective.

Research has proven that adopting good habits is a crucial aspect of health. Crafting lasting and beneficial routines helps healthy actions feel nearly instinctive, generating a continuing process of positive reinforcement. On the flip side, undesirable habits can become ingrained even while they generate negative effects.

Thankfully, humans have an incredible ability to make our behaviors benefit our long-term interests. Building an atmosphere and set of routines that promote our goals can pay off. Sleep hygiene involves both environment and habits, and it can pave the path for higher-quality sleep and greater overall health.

Improving sleep hygiene has little cost and virtually no risk, making it a vital aspect of a public health strategy help fight the significant problems of insufficient sleep and sleeplessness in America.

What Are Signs of Poor Sleep Hygiene?

Having a hard time falling asleep, experiencing frequent sleep interruptions, and enduring daytime tiredness are the most revealing indications of poor sleep hygiene. An overall lack of consistency in sleep amount or quality can also be a marker of poor sleep hygiene.

How Can You Maintain Healthy Sleep Habits?

Having good sleep hygiene is all about setting yourself up for successful sleep each night.

To make healthy sleep seem more effortless, optimize your sleep schedule, pre-bed routine, and daily routines. At the same time, creating a relaxing bedroom atmosphere might serve as a call to unwind and go to sleep. Several recommendations can help in each of these categories, they aren't hard requirements. You can adjust them to meet your circumstances and develop your sleep hygiene checklist to assist achieve the greatest sleep possible. circadian rhythm and limit sleep interruptions.

Get Daylight Exposure: Light, especially sunlight, is one of the primary drivers of circadian rhythms that can encourage excellent sleep.

Be Physically Active: Regular exercise can make it easier to sleep at night and also brings several other health benefits.

Don't Smoke: Nicotine stimulates the body in ways that interrupt sleep, which helps explain why smoking is connected with multiple sleeping difficulties.

Reduce Alcohol Consumption: Alcohol may help you fall asleep faster, but its effects wear off later in the night, disrupting your sleep. Therefore, it's best to limit alcohol intake and abstain from it later in the evening.

Reduce Your Caffeine Consumption in the Afternoon and Evening: Since caffeine is a stimulant, it may keep you awake even while you're trying to sleep. Be careful if you're trying to make up for lack of sleep by drinking a lot of coffee.

Don't Eat Late: Eating dinner later can cause you to still be digesting when it's time for bed, especially if it was a large, filling, or spicy meal. Any meals or snacks eaten before night should generally be on the lighter side.

Limit Activities in Bed: It's advised to just use your bed for sleeping, with sex being the one exception, in order to create a mental association between sleeping and being in bed.

Optimize Your Bedroom

A crucial component of sleep hygiene beyond mere routines is your sleep environment. To fall asleep more quickly, you want your bedroom to emanate peace.

While what makes a bedroom inviting might differ from one person to the next, the following recommendations may help keep it tranquil and free of disruptions:

Have a Comfortable Mattress and Pillow: Your sleeping surface is important for comfort and pain-free sleep, so make an informed decision on the best mattress and pillow for you.

Use Excellent Bedding: The sheets and blankets are the first thing you touch when you get into bed, so it's important to make sure they match your demands and tastes.

Set a Cool Yet Comfortable Temperature: set your bedroom temperature to suit your preferences,

Block Out Light: Use heavy drapes or an eye mask to prevent light from interrupting your sleep.

Drown Out Noise: If you don't find ear plugs comfortable, try a white noise machine or even a fan to drown out distracting noises. Earplugs can help stop noise from keeping you awake.

Try Calming Scents: Light scents, such as lavender, may promote a calmer frame of mind and help cultivate a favorable place for sleep.

Is Sleep Hygiene the Same For Everyone?

The core notion of sleep hygiene that your environment and habits may be modified for better sleep applies to just about everyone, however, what perfect sleep hygiene looks like might vary based on the person.

For that reason, it's important testing out different changes to find out what helps your sleep the most. You don't have to change everything at once; tiny actions can take you toward better sleep hygiene.

Additionally, it's critical to understand that improving sleep hygiene won't always resolve sleeping issues. Better sleep hygiene may help those who experience severe insomnia or other sleep disorders like obstructive sleep apnea, but other therapies are sometimes necessary as well.

In other words, even while it may be useful, sleep hygiene alone isn't a panacea. If you have long-lasting or severe sleeping problems or daytime tiredness, it's advisable to discuss with a doctor who can offer the most effective course of treatment

2. Relaxation techniques

We all endure stressful events throughout our lives, ranging from simple annoyances like traffic jams to more significant anxieties, such as a loved one's critical sickness. It doesn't really matters what causes it, stress floods your body with hormones, which increase your heart rate and how you breathe.

This so-called "stress response" is a normal reaction to dangerous conditions developed in our prehistory to help us withstand hazards like an animal assault or a flood. We rarely confront these physical risks these days, stress response can be kicked of by tough situations of our daily life. Stress response will always be there and we can't all escape it in our life. But we may learn healthy ways of responding to them.

stress symptoms can be lowered through relaxation techniques and help you have a better quality life, especially if you have an ailment such as sleeplessness. Explore relaxation techniques you can practice by yourself.

Relaxation techniques are an excellent strategy to aid with stress management. Relaxation is not just about peace of mind or enjoying a hobby, it's a technique which lowers the effects of stress on your mind and body. Relaxation practices can help you cope with ordinary stress. And these approaches can help with long-term stress or stress associated with various health concerns, such as heart disease and discomfort.

There are various relaxation techniques that the list might be difficult going through, but for the cause of this book, a few will be selected to help you on your path.

Relaxation Exercises To Help With Anxiety And Stress.
guidelines: Before you try relaxation techniques to help you go to sleep, here are some helpful guidelines to keep in mind.

With these exercises, it can be a valuable tools on it own, they may be more beneficial when combined with other exercises to improve your sleep hygiene, which in turn help you in maintaining a consistent sleep schedule and building daytime behaviors that encourage sleep.
Just like mastering any new skill, relaxing exercises take practice. Repetitive and ongoing usage of

relaxation techniques is usually more beneficial than one-time or short-term use.

greatest and most effective relaxation techniques can be tempting to hunt for, finding what works for you, is most important. That may take some experimentation, so if one workout doesn't work, just try another.

While these exercises are safe for most individuals, some may benefit from consulting their doctors before using these procedures. This is particularly crucial for persons with epilepsy, psychiatric problems, or a history of trauma.

How often?
You should aim to set up 20 minutes, 2 or 3 times per day to practice these strategies. The more you practice, the better you will get and the more successful they will be.

It's vital to keep employing these tactics, even if you don't feel better directly away. It will take time and frequent practice before you start to experience the benefits.

preparing yourself

Before you start relaxing, make sure your mind, body, and environment are conducive and ready. To prepare yourself:

Taking off your shoes and putting on comfortable clothes,
select a cool and peaceful area where you'll not be disturbed
lay down or sit comfortably with your legs uncrossed
softly close your eyes, or focus on a location in front of you
declutter your thoughts and focus on your breath
Don't worry if you can't relax instantly. Thoughts could pop into your head. Don't focus on them, simply let them pass through.

Make a note of how relaxed you were before, and after, the exercises to evaluate whether it's helped.

- Meditation
- Colored noise
- Deep breathing
- Progressive muscular relaxation
- Hypnosis
- Visualization
- Body scan

- Meditation

Meditation can be a terrific technique to reduce your pulse rate, focus your attention and also help the brain and body collectively. It doesn't have to be difficult either. The objective of meditation is to calm anxious thoughts and assist you to immerse yourself in the present moment.

But even if you feel your mind straying as you meditate, there's no need to worry. The fact you're taking the effort to work on yourself might be incredibly useful in itself.

Start your meditation

When you're comfy and centered, you can start meditating.

With your eyes closed, simply breathe in while saying "I am calm" in your thoughts as you do. Then breathe out saying "I am calm".

For the following 20 minutes or so, your purpose is to focus on this circular breath and the simple words in your head as much as possible.

It can be tough to focus the thoughts

It's crucial to remember that a wandering mind is a natural element of meditation practice. It's not a failure, only part of learning, and even folks with tons of experience meditating will still have wandering minds sometimes.

The key is to detect when we are sidetracked by a notion and intentionally bring our minds back to focus on the breath.
When you initially start to meditate when your mind wanders, simply thank yourself for noticing.
You then have the opportunity to redirect your focus back to your breath.

Mastering meditation takes practice.
Here's how to tackle some of the obstacles you may face when meditating.

Judging: There is no right or incorrect way to meditate. The key thing is that you have made time to invest in your mental welfare.
A meditation packed with rising thoughts and a wandering mind is still meditation and still effective.

breathing: It might be difficult to find the balance between focusing on the circular breath and breathing spontaneously when meditating.

This is just part of learning the method, so it's necessary to be aware of this as an issue.

Over time you should find the correct mix.

Thoughts: A little thought like paying the electricity bill could grow into anxieties about money or work and take your focus off the meditation.

Remember: having a blank mind is not the purpose of meditation. It's OK if a thought intrudes? simply gently try to move your focus back to your breath.

Bring your meditation to a close

It's important to avoid ending meditation abruptly. When you decide to quit, stop repeating the lines and focus on your breathing, but keep yourself in the same position for a few more minutes with your eyes closed. Open your eyes slowly when you're ready. Before getting up, stay seated for a little while.

Ending a meditation like this allows you a quiet transition into the next section of your day.

- **Colored noise**

Brown noise, often known as red noise, has a bass-like tone and a deeper rumbling sound than pink or white noise. As the frequency increases, the sound level (measured in decibels) decreases more than it does with pink noise. It resembles extended periods of heavy rain or a strong shower. To create a richer, grainier look, some sleep apps use this sound instead of pink noise, which can also be really beneficial to you.

- **Deep breathing**

One of the simplest and most basic ways to activate your body's natural relaxation response is to take slow, deep breaths. Start by taking 10 deep breaths if you're lying in bed awake. Just doing this by itself can start to calm the breath and slow it down. Here are a few different breathing techniques you might try if you're looking for alternatives.

Diaphragmatic Breathing

Diaphragmatic breathing (sometimes termed belly breathing) engages the big muscle at the base of the lungs. Not only may this exercise relieve tension and enhance relaxation, but it can also strengthen the diaphragm and boost the efficiency of our breathing. Here's how to go about it:

While lying down, place one hand on your upper chest and the other hand at the top of your belly, exactly below your rib cage. Your hands will aid to make sure that you're solely breathing through your abdomen during this exercise.

Breathe in through the nose so your stomach presses on your hand, let the other hand, your chest remain as still as possible.

While continuing to maintain your chest motionless, tighten your abdominal muscles and exhale through your lips in a way that you lips looks like you want to blow a whistle

Repeat this process.

Because many of us aren't used to using our diaphragm when we breathe, this exercise may take some practice. Try starting with just a few minutes of diaphragmatic breathing as you get into bed, then gradually increase the time to maximum advantage.

The 3-5-7 Breathing

This slightly more sophisticated breathing method helps manage the speed of your breath. This may not be the ideal option if you're uncomfortable holding your breath, but it's typically regarded as safe and uncomplicated. Here's how it works:

Place the tip of your tongue on the roof of your mouth, directly behind your front teeth (you'll maintain it here for the entire exercise).

Take a deep breath through your nose for about 3 seconds.

Hold the breath for another 5 seconds.

Exhale through your lips for 7 seconds, allowing your exhale to make a natural sound like you're blowing out a candle but gently you don't want to disturb anyone alongside you if there is any.

Just like other breathing exercises, start by practicing this technique for a few minutes before bed. As you get adjusted to the tempo, feel free to increase the time you spend practicing 3-5-7 breathing.

- **Progressive muscular relaxation**

Progressive muscular relaxation techniques depend upon the thought which is difficult to be tense when your muscles are loose. This exercise is performed via cautiously straining and delivering different quantities of individual muscle gatherings, individually.

To begin with, record all of the muscle gatherings or make a sound recording of yourself referencing every one, allowing approximately 45 in the middle of between each gathering to give yourself sufficient opportunity to traverse the strategy.

The muscle bunches incorporate hands, wrists lower arms, biceps, shoulders, temple, around the eyes and nose, cheekbones

Jaw, around the mouth, back of the neck, front of the neck, chest, back, stomach, hips and bottom, thighs, and lower legs

Once you're ready, lie down in bed and attempt the technique:

Close your eyes and let your breathing be your only concentrate. Slowly breathe in through your nose and out through your mouth.
Make a fist, squeezing your hand forcefully.
Hold this for a few seconds, noticing the tension.
Slowly open your fingers and feel the change - notice the tension disappearing. Your hand is more lighter and relaxed. Enjoy this emotion.
If you have any physical injuries or conditions that may cause muscle pain, don't tighten the muscle in that location.

Breathe in and tension the other group of muscles for 5-10 seconds.
Breathe out and immediately relax the muscles in that group.
Stay calm for 10-20 seconds before proceeding to the next muscle group.
Repeat this procedure until you've gone through all the muscle groups. Once you've completed, focus

on retaining all of the muscle groups relaxed as you drift off to sleep.

- **Self-Hypnosis**

Self-hypnosis is similar to progressive muscle relaxation, with the extra step of focusing on a single thought once you're relaxed. The theory is that increasing muscle relaxation puts your body in a hypnotic state, meaning you're relaxed and more open to suggestions.

It can be beneficial to decide on the suggestion you'll utilize before commencing this procedure. Some people focus on a simple word, like relax or let go, while others may repeat a statement like, I'm relaxed and calm. You can even record yourself repeating these sentences and simply listen to them while you're going through progressive muscle relaxation. There are also tapes and DVDs online with pre-recorded phrases for going to sleep.

Once you've settled on your suggestion or phrase, here's how to begin:

Get yourself comfy and recline in bed.

Move into a hypnotic state with a short time of progressive muscle relaxation, tensing and relaxing different muscles in the body.

Once fully calm, carefully repeat your selected phrase.

Once you've mastered self-hypnosis, consider adding in extra sensations to your thought suggestion. Imagine yourself in a safe area and focus on relaxing sights, fragrances, and physical sensations around you. One frequent scenario is envisioning oneself in a field of flowers, smelling nature, and feeling the hottest of the sun on your skin.

- **Visualization**

Visualization Exercises
Another technique to engage the body's natural relaxation response is to use visualization exercises. These strategies rely on employing mental imagery to create a sensation of well-being in the body, which can reduce tension and help you fall asleep.

Imagine your body filled with blue energy or gas, flowing around, filling up every part of you. Imagine this energy reflects your anxieties, tensions, fears, excitement, agitation, and tension.

As you breathe slowly and deeply, visualize gently gathering up all of this energy from your toes, feet, calves, and thighs, starting at the bottom and working your way up feeling each area of your lower body relax as the energy exits. Envision pushing the blue gas up from your lower body into your stomach area, where it accumulates into an energy ball.

While proceeding to inhale profoundly, envision gradually hauling the blue energy from your fingertips, hands, arms, shoulders, and down into your stomach, allowing it to join the others, delivering a much more prominent bundle of blue energy. Presently, your arms and hands are feeling loose.

Keep breathing, and bring the energy down from your head, neck, and chest and add it to the turning chunk of blue energy that presently fills your stomach region. Feel loosened up in your chest area and head.

This chunk of blue energy presently holds everything, each of your nerves, pressures, and fears. As you gradually and completely breathe in and breathe out, envision impacting the energy ball out of the highest point of your head, through the structure, outside, and straight out of sight. Watch it go past the tree tops, through the mists, and into space like a falling star.

Feel your body loose and serene. Presently, you're prepared to rest.

- **Body Scan**

Body scans are a sort of meditation that entails gradual, focused attention to different parts of the body. Once you're lying comfortably in bed, attempt these steps for a soothing body scan:

Start by taking a few deep breaths, possibly trying diaphragmatic or 3-5-7 breathing, to get your body into a relaxed position.

Bring your attention to your feet, notice any feelings in your toes, and if you're carrying any stress in this part of the body.

If you detect discomfort here, acknowledge it and attempt to let go of whatever ideas or stories you have. Visualize the stress leaving the body through the breath.

When you're ready, switch your concentration to your calf muscles, repeating the process of detecting sensations, letting go of thoughts or tales, and envisioning the tension leaving through your breath.

Methodically transfer your focus to each portion of your body, one by one, moving from your feet to your forehead until you've scanned your entire body.

After relaxation
Don't rush to get up following relaxation exercises. Sit with your eyes closed for a few minutes to avoid the danger of feeling dizzy. Open your eyes and make sure you feel alright before rising.

Chapter Four

Sleep logs

Sleep logs, also known as sleep diaries or sleep journals, records that you keep to document various elements of your sleep patterns and behaviors. These diaries are important tools for tracking sleep quality, finding trends, and providing valuable information to healthcare experts when examining sleep difficulties or disorders. Here's a tutorial on creating and using sleep logs effectively:

Components of a Sleep Log:

Bedtime and Wake Time: Record the time you go to bed and the time you wake up each day. This helps establish your sleep duration.

Sleep Quality: Rate the quality of your sleep on a scale, often ranging from poor to great. This can help you uncover patterns between sleep quality and other factors.

Naps: Note any daytime naps and their durations. Napping can affect nighttime sleep, therefore it's crucial to watch them as well.

Sleep Environment: Describe your sleep environment, including things like room temperature, noise level, and lighting settings.

Activities Before Bed: Document any activities you engage in before night, such as reading, watching TV, using electronic devices, or consuming coffee.

Food and Drink: Note the types and amounts of food and beverages taken in the hours leading up to bedtime, as certain meals and drinks can affect sleep.

Stress and Mood: Record your stress levels and mood before night. Stress and emotional condition can influence sleep quality.

Medications and Supplements: List any medications or supplements you use, as they can impair sleep.

Using Sleep Logs:

Consistency: make sure to fill up your sleep journal every day for at least a couple of weeks. Consistency is necessary to discern patterns and trends accurately.

Tracking: Look for patterns in your sleep data. Are there specific activities or factors that tend to influence your sleep quality positively or negatively?

Identifying Issues: Sleep logs can help you and healthcare experts discover any sleep problems or habits that can be harming your sleep.

Adjustments: Based on the information from your sleep diary, you can make informed adjustments to your sleep pattern, environment, or behaviors to improve your sleep quality.

Communication: If you're seeking help for sleep-related concerns, sharing your sleep journal with a healthcare expert can provide valuable information for diagnosis and therapy recommendations.

Provide specific details about your sleep experience, such as the time you went to bed, the number of times you woke up during the night, and any variables that might have contributed to your sleep quality.

Chapter Five

Addressing the problem

Now let's put insomnia where it belongs, have in mind that a problem like insomnia won't just leave you instantly, it's just like you building your body, you can't go to the gym and on the first day expect to see changes rather what you will get is pain, I mean lots of pain that will discourage you from going back there, but when you remember why you have to go to the guy, well you mind will automatically tell your body that the pain is just temporary that the result is what you're looking at. The same principle applies here when you start implementing what is in this book, you will be discouraged cause you might not get results in your first week, but you will start seeing results but not the way you expected them to be, all you need is consistency, believe and have positive thoughts that you have finally put your problem where it belongs.

once you address these few problems, you'll be able to fall asleep effortlessly, sleep deeply, and wake up feeling rested and rejuvenated every day, your anxiety, worry, fear, and frustration about your sleep will disappear and you'll feel calm, and confident about your ability to sleep and sleep well every night for the rest of your life your focus sharpness energy and your vitality will return during the day so you can function at the highest level in your work and in your life you're going to feel like yourself again and be fully present with the people and activities you most enjoy and care about your energy health and your happiness and your zest for life will quickly return sleep and to sleep well and you'll be able to sleep naturally and healthily for the rest of your life

Now let's look at these few measures in Which we will be talking for you to get your desired results and send sleeplessness farewell for good

Five simple steps to conquering insomnia

Step 1. Your Mindset

Human thoughts, sentiments, and ways of behaving are moored in the mind, where a complicated organization of cells gets data from the inside and outer climate, making an interpretation of this data into our experience of ourselves, our general surroundings, and our associations with it.

The way the brain is wired

The HMM is predicated upon the assumption that the brain is constituted of distinct components that have different functions and that communicate information in a hierarchical, integrated fashion. For example, there are areas of the brain that are responsible for processing sensory stimuli and governing particular types of movement, while other parts of the brain, such as the prefrontal cortex, integrate and act upon information acquired elsewhere to make executive decisions.

The human mind is a sophisticated and comprehensive mechanism responsible for processing thoughts, emotions, perceptions, memories, and conscious awareness. It encompasses many cognitive activities and operates in cooperation with the brain and body to govern physiological responses and behaviors.

1. Mind-Body Connection:
The mind and body are intertwined and continually impact each other. This relationship is commonly referred to as the mind-body connection. The mind can affect the body through both conscious and subconscious processes, and the body's state can, in turn, impact mental and emotional well-being.

2. Psychological Effects on the Body:

The mind may dramatically alter the body's physiological processes and functioning. For example:

Stress Response: Psychological pressures cause the body's stress response, which involves the release of stress hormones including cortisol and adrenaline. This response can lead to increased heart rate, heightened attention, and muscle tension.

Emotional experiences can alter heart rate, blood pressure, digestion, and immune function. Positive emotions can enhance well-being, whereas negative emotions can contribute to physical tension and discomfort.

Beliefs and expectations can alter bodily reactions. The placebo effect reveals gains in health due to positive thoughts, while the nocebo effect can lead to unfavorable consequences due to negative ideas or expectations.

Emotional anguish can show as physical symptoms without a clear medical reason. For instance, stress can contribute to headaches, stomach difficulties, and weariness.

3. How the Mind Influences the Body's Reactions:
The mind controls the body's behavior through different mechanisms:

Neurotransmitters: Thoughts and emotions lead to the release of neurotransmitters in the brain. For example, pleasant thoughts can induce the release of "feel-good" neurotransmitters like serotonin.

Emotional experiences induce the release of hormones that alter physical functioning. Fear can lead to the release of stress hormones, whereas enjoyment can increase the release of endorphins.

The mind plays a role in regulating the autonomic nervous system, which controls involuntary body functions like heart rate, digestion, and breathing rate. The sympathetic branch initiates the "fight or flight" response, whereas the parasympathetic branch encourages relaxation.
Signals from the brain pass through neural pathways to various sections of the body, influencing physical reactions. For example, stress signals can lead to muscle tension and a higher heart rate.

4. Mind-Body Practices:

Mind-body techniques like meditation, deep breathing, and biofeedback use the mind-body link to enhance relaxation and well-being. These techniques can regulate physiological reactions, reduce stress, and increase general health.

Understanding the delicate relationship between the mind and body is vital for promoting holistic health. Cultivating happy ideas, reducing stress, and practicing mindfulness can contribute to a balanced mind-body connection and improve general well-being.

mind has a key and important function in the therapy of insomnia. Since insomnia generally involves a combination of psychological and physiological issues, addressing the psychological part through various treatments is vital for improving sleep quality. The mind's influence on thoughts, emotions, and behaviors can greatly impact sleep patterns and habits. Here's how the mind contributes to the therapy of insomnia:

Cognitive Behavioral Therapy for Insomnia (CBT-I): CBT-I is a highly successful psychological treatment for insomnia. It focuses on recognizing and altering mental patterns, beliefs, and actions that lead to sleep disorders. The mind's role in this treatment involves:

Cognitive Restructuring: Challenging and modifying negative beliefs and fears about sleep that might prolong insomnia.

Stimulus Control: Re-establishing the relationship between the bed and sleep, and breaking associations between the bed and alertness.

Sleep Restriction: Restricting the time spent in bed to match actual sleep duration, therefore boosting sleep efficiency.

Relaxation Techniques: Teaching relaxation ways to soothe the mind and body before sleep.

Mindfulness and Relaxation Techniques: Mindfulness meditation, deep breathing, progressive muscle relaxation, and other relaxation techniques can help calm the mind, reduce stress, and prepare the body for sleep.

Stress and Anxiety Management: Addressing underlying stressors and anxieties that lead to sleeplessness is vital. Learning stress management skills and coping strategies can help individuals manage racing thoughts and worries that often interfere with falling asleep.

Sleep Hygiene Education: Educating folks on good sleep habits and routines empowers them to build a sleep-conducive atmosphere and establish consistent pre-sleep rituals that tell the mind that it's time to wind down.

Sleep Education: Understanding the normal sleep-wake cycle and the importance of the circadian rhythm can help individuals match their daily routines and habits with their body's internal clock.

Relaxing Bedtime Routine: Engaging in relaxing activities before bed, such as reading, taking a warm bath, or practicing relaxation exercises, can help ease the mind and encourage a smoother transition to sleep.

Limiting Stimulants: Avoiding caffeine, cigarettes, and stimulating activities close to bedtime helps prevent the mind from being overly awake when it's time to wind down.

Addressing Sleep Anxiety: The mind's fear of not sleeping can generate a cycle of concern that perpetuates insomnia. Learning to manage and reframe these anxious thoughts is a vital element of treatment.

Sleep Diary and Monitoring: Keeping a sleep diary helps individuals track their sleep habits, identify triggers, and assess progress during the treatment process.

In summary, the mind's function in the therapy of insomnia is to address psychological problems that contribute to sleep difficulties. By altering thought patterns, regulating stress and anxiety, and adopting healthy sleep routines, you can favorably improve your sleep quality and overcome insomnia. Relaxing the mind is a critical stage in preparation for a good night's sleep. Calming the mind helps minimize tension, worry, and racing thoughts that might interfere with going asleep and staying asleep

Step 2. Understanding the real cause

The underlying reason for sleeplessness can be varied and differs from individual to person. It's generally a combination of physical, psychological, and environmental variables that contribute to sleep issues. Identifying the underlying cause of insomnia is critical for effective therapy. Let's discuss the few elements that genuinely produces these problem, once you grasp these reason you will also know how to put them in check

Physical Factors:
Chronic Pain: Physical discomfort or pain can make it difficult to find a comfortable sleeping position and stay asleep, lots of physical pain does arise at night and can be severe depending on the type of the injury.
Medical Conditions: Various health conditions, such as asthma, allergies, and gastrointestinal issues, can cause discomfort and impair sleep.
Hormonal Changes: Fluctuations in hormones due to menstruation, pregnancy, or menopause might impact sleep patterns.
Sleep Disorders: Conditions including sleep apnea, restless legs syndrome, and periodic limb movement disorder can disturb sleep quality.

Chronic Illness: Conditions like diabetes, heart disease, and neurological issues can impair sleep.

drugs: Some drugs have insomnia as a side effect, or they can influence sleep-wake rhythms.

Substance Use: Alcohol, caffeine, and certain recreational drugs might interfere with sleep.

Age-related Changes: Changes in sleep architecture and hormone levels as people age might impair sleep quality.

Neurological Conditions: Conditions including anxiety, sadness, and schizophrenia can alter sleep patterns.

Psychological Factors:

Stress and Anxiety: Psychological stressors cause the body's stress response, Emotional stress, worry, and anxiety are key contributors to sleeplessness. Racing thoughts and excessive concern might make it difficult to relax and fall asleep.

Depression: Depressive symptoms can disturb sleep, leading to sleeplessness or excessive drowsiness.

Anxiety Disorders: Conditions like generalized anxiety disorder and post-traumatic stress disorder can contribute to persistent worry and sleep difficulties.

Racing Thoughts: Persistent, racing thoughts and excessive worry might make it tough to relax and fall asleep.

Trauma: Past traumatic experiences can contribute to nightmares, night sweats, and trouble sleeping.

Environmental Factors:

Sleep Environment: Noise, light, an uncomfortable mattress, and an incorrect room temperature, a cluttered or disordered sleep environment can impair sleep quality.

Electronic Devices: Exposure to the blue light emitted by electronic devices before night can interfere with the generation of melatonin, a sleep-inducing hormone.

Work Schedule: Shift work, irregular work hours, or night shifts can interrupt the body's natural sleep-wake cycle.

Travel and Time Zones: Rapid travel across time zones might lead to jet lag and temporary sleep difficulties.

Sleep Environment: can add to stress and impair sleep.

All these conditions listed above induce Negative Thought Patterns. Negative mental habits concerning sleep, such as

dread of not sleeping,

I only slept 5 hours yesterday night
I've lost my sleeping capacity
I felt like garbage yesterday because I didn't get enough sleep
I won't be able to function adequately tomorrow if I don't get enough sleep

These things lead to insomnia, they first lead to poor sleep. Poor sleep is merely one or a few nights of difficulty sleeping which is natural, it happens to everybody. It's not sleeplessness, at least not yet, and at that time there's no problem.

Once the stress, the initial trigger here has been taken care of the poor sleep will go away and you get adequate sleep and your sleep goes back to normal.

But what produces insomnia is when someone gets that initial poor sleep they start having negative thoughts in reaction those create anxiety and worry and tension and aggravation around your sleep
Sometimes it's called sleep anxiety or sleep worry and then that drives you to desire to do something about it because you're worried you're thinking.
what's happening, there's something wrong with my sleep, I better do something about this and then the things that you do or that most people do end up

messing up their sleep even more and making it worse, and of course, you're doing this unwittingly, you're doing it trying to assist your sleep but it's affecting your sleep these are called negative sleep habits

Over time if you keep changing those behaviors around your sleep it's going to lead to more poor sleep which is going to lead to more negative thoughts patterns, like anxiety frustration hopelessness which is going to lead to you engaging in more negative sleep behaviors and then over time this cycle just continues until it doesn't stop and it just keeps spinning around, creating the insomnia cycle

And once you're in this cycle even once the initial trigger that caused the poor sleep even once that's resolved and it's not there anymore, the insomnia over here will continue because now it is its problem now it has moved your entire physiology and sleep system and it's now a separate problem that has to be addressed at the root

So insomnia is produced by negative thought patterns in response to the poor sleep and negative sleep behaviors in response to the poor sleep and the negative thought patterns and the worry that you should do something to improve your sleep which then produces additional difficulties with the sleep.

So to eradicate insomnia you need to fully adjust your negative thoughts patterns and your negative sleep practices which are the foundation of the problem

Now let's address the negative thoughts patterns.
so what are negative thoughts patterns, like I indicated earlier, things like I'm dreading bedtime
I must get eight hours of sleep
I won't be able to function tomorrow if
I don't sleep well tonight
I only slept four hours last night thus I
won't be able to function or do well in
my career or be a decent parent today
I've lost my ability to sleep
I had a poor night of sleep and I'm going to feel like garbage today

These are frequent negative thinking patterns or anxieties about sleep that become created and these are a natural aspect of insomnia everyone that has insomnia has these negative thoughts patterns, fears, and anxiety around their sleep

And the point is these things may look like typical responses to insomnia but they make insomnia worse so they seem normal because when you have insomnia you are in reality not sleeping well you're having horrible nights of sleep you don't feel well the next day it is a problem that you're having.

and so it seems reasonable to believe bad things about it but this is the cycle that develops the negative mental patterns which lead to anxiety fear frustration stress

All of these emotions are very stimulating and they wake you up so if you're having these before you go to bed or you're having them in bed when you're struggling to sleep, they stimulate you they wake you up they have the opposite of the effect that you want and then that causes trouble sleeping and then that puts you right into that cycle because now then you have more worry because your sleep is not getting better and it's getting worse
therefore you need to address this straight at the root which comes from the negative thinking patterns, if you don't change your negative thoughts patterns then the cycle just continues and continues and will likely become worse over time

How do you change negative thought patterns?

well to shift your beliefs around your sleep and insomnia you need to recognize, change and replace negative thoughts patterns with more accurate adaptive, positive thoughts patterns and there's a particular way to do this, it is not like doing positive affirmations which don't work it's about shifting it to positive beliefs that are 100 percent true that resonate with you and that shift from the negative to the more positive

what promotes negative thoughts are the many myths and erroneous beliefs that individuals hold about sleep and insomnia that regrettably leads to worry, frustration, despair, and hopelessness.

So to erase those you need to learn the facts regarding sleep and insomnia and these facts are based on

Keeping a positive attitude.
Accept that there are things that may likely happen and you will have no control over them.
Be forceful instead of being aggressive. Assert your feelings, thoughts, or beliefs instead of getting angry, defensive, or passive.
Learn to manage your time more successfully.

Set limits correctly and say no to requests that might bring excessive stress to your life.
Make time for the things that interest you and hobbies as well.

So you have to identify the genuine cause, because if you do not address the source, the Negative Thought Patterns enter in leading to bad sleep patterns and this eats your sleeping time which will lead to insomnia.

Once this source is treated you will stop having a Negative mind pattern.
You will sense peace, self-confidence, and undoubtedly sleep better and wake up rejuvenated.
Now let's talk about the next step

Step 3. Make your bed a place to sleep.

The thoughts we focus on can have a big impact on how well we sleep. You can't see your bed as a nighttime battlefield and expect to find serenity there; how is that possible? Our ideas, emotions, and mental activity play a key role in the process of falling asleep.

It can be difficult to relax if your mind is engaged with stress, worry, or anxiety, which can enhance physiological arousal. Stress chemicals like cortisol, which are released by the body in reaction to anxious thoughts, might prevent the body from falling asleep naturally.

Before night, racing thoughts will keep your mind active and delay the beginning of sleep by engaging in interesting mental activities. It's crucial to visualize your bed as a place to sleep so that your mind can imagine it as a place of rest.

It might be difficult for your body to wind down for sleep when you are focused on stimulating or exciting activities, such as heated conversations, action-packed movies, or playing competitive video games.

Let's discuss what it means. At the moment, your bed and your bedroom are linked to restlessness, worry, annoyance, and terror. Your bed has essentially turned into a foe of sleep rather than a place to welcome a weary body in need of rest.

Even if you feel worn out and you haven't slept, there are many people who literally feel like they are going into combat every night when they go to bed. Perhaps you have also experienced it. well, in a few days, weeks, or even months years for some individuals, the moment you climb into bed, you jolt awake and whether you're awake or have that strange feeling, lack of sleep

What the heck is happening, then? The reason is that you've put in so much time. During nights spent tossing and turning in bed, becoming irritated and concerned that your sleeping surroundings, such as your bed and your bedroom, have changed into an area for awake and arousal

For instance, if you walk into your kitchen, you're likely to start thinking about food right away. You might get hungry or start considering eating because that's what you do in the kitchen and what you've done countless times throughout your life, so those two things are connected. The kitchen is now a place for all of those things.

The same thing happens with insomnia; your brain associates not sleeping but being awake and anxious with the bed because if you've spent many hours, many days, or weeks in that state it confuses your brain and now the bed becomes a trigger. For many people, the smell of that buttered popcorn cooking has become associated with a movie theater because you've experienced that so many times it gets associated in your brain.

The bed is a strong place for sleep for good sleepers or normal sleepers, right? Perhaps your partner is one of these good sleepers. Perhaps you once were someone like that, where you got into bed and instead of feeling more alert and awake, you just felt sleepy and fell asleep within minutes, like it knocked you out. Basically, poor sleepers are people with insomnia. The bed has turned into a strong place for wakefulness, and that's one important factor that keeps insomnolence from getting
Therefore, we need to break this tendency by making the bed a place where you can fall asleep easily and enjoyably rather than waking up as soon as your head strikes the pillow.

Making your bed a place to sleep is the secret weapon because it will radically change how your body reacts to getting into bed from how it currently does.

The way to do this is to give your sleep structure. Right now, you don't have any structure, and your sleep is disorganized because you're engaging in one or more of the negative sleep behaviors I mentioned earlier. What are those negative sleep behaviors? They include things like sleeping in, you had a really bad night of sleep, but you have the option of sleeping in, so you do, or it could also mean going to bed early.

All of these factors contribute to insomnia even if you're doing them to help you sleep because you're worried about your sleep, which prevents you from falling asleep. You might also have taken sleeping pills, supplements, or other drugs, not everyone does this, but it's another bad sleep habit that worsens things. Alternatively, you might be trying extremely hard to fall asleep. We'll discuss this issue in more detail in the next step.

The thing about insomnia is that it throws your sleep off course. Instead of following the path of a strong, regular pattern, it gets thrown off course by the things we discussed, the negative sleep behaviors, and negative thought patterns, and that cycle throws your sleep onto a different track. Some people have never experienced really good, normal, healthy sleep, but many people have.

The strategies and processes work to move it off the present bad track and back on the usual track, therefore you must cease doing them if you want to give your sleep a constant and healthy structure.

Rumination, which keeps your mind active and prevents relaxation, is caused by dwelling on unpleasant feelings, unresolved problems, or emotional anguish. To avoid this, attempt to send a clear signal to your brain that you are going to rest and nothing else.

Improving sleep quality requires creating a sleep-friendly environment.
Even on weekends, going to bed and waking up at the same time each day can assist your body's internal clock to stay in check and will help you associate your bed with sleep.

Create a relaxing pre-sleep ritual that you follow before going to bed. This regimen could involve reading, using relaxation techniques, or doing light stretches. By doing this, you're telling your mind that your bedroom is beckoning, which will cause it to crave your bed and, ultimately, cause you to think only about sleeping.

You should only use your bed for sleeping and private activities. Avoid performing tasks that could disrupt the connection between your bed and sleep, such as working, studying, or using electronic devices in bed.

Before going to bed, rather than once in bed, practice relaxation techniques like deep breathing, meditation, or progressive muscle relaxation. This aids in cognitive relaxation and sends a signal to the body that it is time to wind down.

As you get ready for the night, turn down the lights in your bedroom. Melatonin is a hormone that helps people go to sleep, and lowering the lighting can cause its release.

Make sure your bedding, pillows, and mattress are cozy and favorable to sleeping. Spend money on luxurious bedding that encourages comfort and relaxation.

Keep the temperature in your bedroom at a pleasant level. A cooler room temperature often makes for better sleep.

Reduce noise interference in your bedroom. To block out outside noises, try using earplugs or think about using a white noise machine.

Create a calming environment by employing aromatherapy to diffuse sleep-inducing scents like lavender or chamomile. In order to reduce light and create a dark sleeping environment, you can also use blackout curtains.

Disconnect from Work because your body may take some time to recognize that you want to sleep if you are not mentally clear of work or other stressful activities before bed. You can make the transition from a hectic day to a quiet night by engaging in relaxing activities.

Try writing down any anxieties or ideas in a journal before going to sleep if your mind is prone to racing. This can aid in mental acuity and stop ruminating.

Consistency is important, keep this in mind. Your bed will eventually come to represent sleep in your mind, which will make it simpler for you to unwind and drift off while you are lying down. After 20 to 30 minutes, if you still can't fall asleep, it's advised that you get out of bed and do something calming until you nod off. You can get a lot of sleep by picking a dull book to read.

Make your bed a sleeping cue with these four essential sleeping habits.

1. You should keep track of how much time you spend in bed because you should only use the mattress to sleep or make love and not for other purposes. This will help you distinguish between the time you spend sleeping and the time you actually spend in bed.

2. while you are sleeping at night
Your body and mind have the chance to rest and regenerate when you go to bed at night. Your sleeping patterns and nighttime activities can have a big impact on how you feel the next morning.

3. What you do when awake also counts; get out of bed and attempt some mental activity, like the earlier-discussed meditation.

4. Instead of hurrying to do your daily tasks as soon as you wake up, ask yourself if you are refreshed, whether you got enough sleep, and what else you can do to preserve or improve your sleep. Give your body a few minutes to properly awaken.

Whenever possible during the day, go outside to get some vitamin D and sunlight.

Step 4. Effortlessly induce sleep

One of the sources of insomnia is the effort to sleep. So let me begin by noting that efforts in general are a totally natural thing; they are the result of our internal problem-solving processes, which are how we get things done. Therefore, anytime we encounter a difficulty, an issue, or a goal, our brain employs this system to find the optimal answer and fulfill the objective; without it, we would not be able to perform many of the things we do. This is a typical and helpful technique in general, but when it comes to sleep, it is less effective because sleep functions a little bit differently than other problems.

So picture sleep as the absence of light. By analogy with the darkness, sleep is the absence of attention awareness. When we sleep, we are not in focus; we are not actively thinking about something. Because it is an unconscious process that cannot be controlled and is passive, it follows that we actually don't need to do anything in order to fall asleep. Thus, the opposite side is making genuine attempts. In other words, when we try to improve our sleep, we actually put a lot of consciousness into sleep, which is an unconscious process, and as a result, sleep disappears, so the less we try to improve our sleep, the better. Attention is consciousness; it is focused on something, on achieving something, and when we are doing any sort of effort we are very much aware of things we are solving.

I divided them into three main groups. Thus, efforts and acts fall under the first group. We take highly proactive measures to manage our sleep, like this. For instance, we might decide to get dark curtains or start taking specialized pills like melatonin or vitamin C or something. By doing this, we truly contribute something to our routine by acting particularly in a particular way. The action-based effort is the second kind. Usually, avoidant conduct looks like this.

coffee, staying away from certain items, such as blue light after dark, or changing your plans

The third problematic category is effort thoughts, which might be conversations with friends in the evening or other such activities. It is typically our attempt to think about the right ideas, such as forcing ourselves to think positively or telling ourselves self-affirmations in an effort to improve our sleep, or it could be our attempt to resist getting rid of specific thoughts that we consider wrong. For instance,

Try not to consider sleeping. With those three approaches, we try to block off thoughts of anxiousness and, you know, close our ears and act as though this isn't occurring. The query is:

Once they are discovered, what do we actually do with them? There are three possible approaches here. When you recognize that you are about to perform anything with intent, the first one is typically like discarding the effort. to induce sleep, you often choose

Don't do it at all. Let's imagine you decide to take some vitamins because you believe they will help you sleep better.

Tomorrow or today, I won't be taking it.

The second option, which is very similar to the first, is to take the opposite action.

But here, we're kind of increasing this effect of doing, which is the difference.

the exact opposite, so let's say you are avoiding coffee and then decide to purposefully face your fear by downing two cups of coffee. As a result, you sort of demonstrate your boldness and bravery.

You tell your brain, "Okay, I'm not going to be scared by you," and as a result, you just do the thing that makes you the most anxious.

The third technique to engage with efforts is to just acknowledge them, which entails being aware of them without taking any action. It particularly works with efforts and thoughts, so if you have a thought and then have an intention, either to get rid of it or to simply make yourself think in a particular manner, you just accept that, "Okay, I'm just doing that, and this is an effort."

These three approaches are what I used in my personal journey; of course, you get to choose which one you want to employ for yourself. effort and you choose not to react, as in not taking action. It might be more direct or gentler, like the third approach, which is simply noting it without responding to it and, frequently, consulting your own feelings: Just go with whatever makes you comfortable.

Step 5. Speak with someone.

Coaching

If you're reading this book and you're on this page, it indicates you're experiencing severe sleep issues that you haven't been able to resolve on your own. You've seen an overview of what's causing and perpetuating your insomnia and the important stages of eliminating it.

Since insomnia is a serious issue that won't go away on its own and is wholly unneeded, you should make it your top goal to find a solution. You can get rid of insomnia no matter how long you've battled it or what you've tried, and you can maintain a regular, healthy sleep pattern for the rest of your life. However, you're unlikely to be able to do this on your own; in fact, the methods you've used to get better sleep have likely contributed to and are still contributing to your insomnia. This is what we've discussed.

You, therefore, need a coach to guide you through the process because there are numerous issues that must be addressed in precisely the proper manner in order to achieve success. Sleep influences every function in your body, so when you don't get enough sleep, it has an impact on every aspect of your life.

If you don't find a solution to this issue, your sleeplessness may last for years or even decades. I'm not telling you this to scare you, but it's true that some people struggle with insomnia for years or even decades despite there being no justifiable cause.

There are many benefits to investing and coaching. It offers a straightforward, step-by-step process for success, prevents overwhelm and confusion, and lowers anxiety, uncertainty, worry, and stress related to sleep because you aren't trying to figure this out on your own, which may be difficult for most people to do.

You receive expert help on how to modify and customize the process for you, your insomnia, and your sleep system after learning the proper order and timing for precisely how and when to apply each of the strategies.

Support and accountability are essential components of the process since they let you know what to do and when you need to know it most.

You just need that moral support while you're struggling.

Therefore, this is how coaching works: it begins with your mindset, your beliefs about what is possible, and your beliefs about your sleep and insomnia. This is the fundamental thing you must do first because it puts you in the right frame of mind to be able to overcome insomnia and go through the process. The second is the actual method you use to overcome insomnia, and the results from that healthy, high-quality sleep for life and your happiness come next.

Chapter Six

Relapse prevention

1. controlling daytime anxiety

The ability to control daily stress is crucial for general health and can have a big impact on how well you sleep at night. Here are some practical tips to assist you in controlling midday stress:

meditate in the present moment or practice deep breathing. These methods can assist you in maintaining awareness, lowering your level of anxiety, and encouraging calm.

Every day, set aside a little period of time to relax, pay attention to your breathing and put your racing thoughts to rest.

Physical Exercise:

Exercise on a regular basis to release endorphins and lower stress chemicals.

Whether you prefer dancing, yoga, jogging, or walking, pick an activity you enjoy. Try to exercise most days of the week for at least 30 minutes.

Management of time:

Make a daily timetable and prioritize your duties to prevent feeling overloaded.

Focus on one item at a time and divide activities into smaller, more manageable chunks.
Habits of a Healthy Lifestyle:

Consume a healthy diet that is high in whole grains, lean proteins, and fruits and vegetables.
Sugar and caffeine in excess can cause energy swings and tension, so stay away from them.
Keep hydrated

Make sure you're drinking enough water throughout the day as dehydration can make stress worse.
Embrace the outdoors:

Spend time outside, whether you're relaxing in a garden or taking a quick stroll around a park. The presence of nature might help to quiet the mind.
Relaxation techniques to practice:

To relieve physical strain, try practicing progressive muscle relaxation, in which you contract and then release various muscular groups.
Use visualization to your advantage by picturing a calm, soothing setting for yourself.
Social Assistance:

Join up with your loved ones, friends, or a support group. Emotional relief might result from discussing your feelings with a trusted friend or family member.
Decrease Screen Time:

Set limits on your screen usage, especially when it comes to social media and the news, which can increase your stress.
Think about taking breaks from technology to let your mind rest.
Have Fun and Laugh:

Take part in enjoyable pursuits, such as viewing a funny movie or spending time with close friends and family.
Interests and Originality:

Take up a hobby you like, whether it's gardening, playing an instrument, or painting. An effective way to reduce stress is through creativity.
Develop Your Gratitude:

Keep a thankfulness diary where you can record the things you are grateful for every day. Your viewpoint may change if you concentrate on the positives.
Keep in mind that stress management during the day is a continual effort. Try out a few different

approaches to see which one suits you the best. These routines can help you develop resilience and lead a more tranquil and balanced daily life over time.

2. keep up a healthy way of life

The incidence of sleeplessness can be considerably decreased or prevented by leading a healthy lifestyle. In your lifestyle, pay attention to the following:

Regular Sleep Schedule:
Even on weekends, go to bed and get up at the same time every day. Consistency aids in regulating your body's biological clock, making it simpler to naturally go to sleep and wake up.
Establish a peaceful bedtime routine:

Create a relaxing bedtime ritual that includes things like reading, light stretching, meditation, or having a warm bath. Your body will receive this signal and know it's time to relax.
Environment That Promotes Sleep:

Make your bedroom a cozy place for sleeping. Make sure you have comfortable bedding, pillows,

and mattresses. Temperature, noise, and light disturbances should all be adjusted.
Avoid using screens right before bed:

At least an hour before going to bed, stay away from electronic devices with screens (phones, tablets, computers). Screens' blue light can prevent the body from producing melatonin.
Drinking water and eating mindfully:

Avoid eating large, spicy, or heavy meals right before bed because they can make you uncomfortable. Reduce fluid intake in the evening as well to reduce midnight awakenings for bathroom visits.
Physical Exercise:

Regular physical activity is recommended, but avoid strenuous exercise right before night. Better sleep can be facilitated by regular exercise, but strenuous activity late in the day may be stimulating.
a balanced diet

Eat a healthy, balanced diet that is high in fruits, vegetables, whole grains, and lean proteins. Avoid consuming too much coffee and sweets, especially in the hours before night.

Stress Reduction:
Use stress-reduction methods including progressive muscle relaxation, deep breathing, mindfulness, and meditation. Taking care of your stress during the day can help you unwind at night.
Limiting nicotine and alcohol:

Avoid consuming too much alcohol and nicotine, especially right before bed. While alcohol may help you feel sleepy at first, it can interfere with sleep later in the night.
Daytime Light Exposure:
During the day, expose yourself to natural sunshine. Natural light exposure can enhance the quality of your sleep while regulating your body's circadian rhythm.
Establish a Daytime Schedule:
Create a daily schedule that incorporates work, meals, exercise, and leisure pursuits. Better sleep patterns can result from a sense of order.
Having a positive outlook and relaxing:

Take part in enjoyable and relaxing activities throughout the day. Overall well-being can be enhanced by indulging in hobbies, practicing mindfulness, and spending time with loved ones.
By including these healthy lifestyle practices in your daily routine, you may foster a setting that

encourages sound sleep and lowers the chance of insomnia. Keep in mind that tiny adjustments made over time can have a significant influence on your health overall and quality of sleep.
the capacity to sleep.

When should I seek care and when should I visit my doctor?
If you discover that your insomnia lasts for more than a few nights or if it starts to interfere with your everyday activities, duties, and routines, you should speak with your healthcare practitioner (preferably a primary care provider). Also, if you see any of the following, you should speak with them:

Sleepiness that is difficult to fight during the day.
Microsleeps are brief periods of time when you nod off while awake, especially if they take place when you're working or driving.
if you suffer from any other conditions that impact how much or how well you sleep, such as mental health issues.
What inquiries ought I to make of my physician?
Does my physical health have an impact on how well I sleep? Are there any symptoms I might have that prevent me from falling asleep?
What effects are my drugs having on my sleep, if any?

What should I do if I believe that my mental health is preventing me from falling asleep?

Maintain a positive outlook.

Recognize that some things are beyond your control.

Instead of being aggressive, be forceful. Instead of being irate, defensive, or passive, express your feelings, opinions, or beliefs.

Improve your time management skills.

Set reasonable boundaries and refuse requests that would put too much stress on your life.

Make time for your interests and hobbies.

Avoid using drugs, alcohol, or compulsive habits as a way to cope with stress. Alcohol and drug use might cause your body even more stress.

Look for social assistance. Give your loved ones enough time.

To discover more healthy ways to handle the stress in your life, seek counseling from a psychologist or other mental health expert experienced in stress management or biofeedback techniques.

Conclusion

Take a minute to consider your experience as our trip through the worlds of sleep and wakefulness comes to an end. You have descended into the depths of the night, prepared with knowledge and a goal. You've cut the tangles of unrest, replacing them with a tapestry of calm and renewal.

Every time you turn a page, you add to your toolbox of tricks and methods for controlling your racing thoughts, calming your troubled emotions, and invoking peaceful slumber. You've listened to accounts of people who have won their own struggles with sleep deprivation and been motivated by their successes.

But keep in mind that this is not a journey that comes to an end when a book is finished. Every time you go to sleep at night, the journey doesn't end. The companions that will lead you to the serene shores of sleep are the wisdom you have gained, the rituals you have adopted, and the newfound control you have over your sleeping surroundings.

You may change your nights and change the plot of your sleep tale as you move forward, equipped with your newly discovered insights. The nights don't necessarily have to be a place of conflict; they can also be a haven, a place of safety from the tumult of the day. Accept the night, accept the dream, and allow the healing dance of sleep to do its work.

May you find comfort in the arms of sound sleep as the stars overhead lullaby you and the moon bathes you in its soft glow. Recognize that you have the power to open the doors to peaceful evenings, where every breath is a note of tranquility and every dream is a stroke of possibility.

As a result, dear dreamer, go off on your journey and allow the lessons you acquire from these pages to lead you to mornings of regenerated vitality and nights of profound sleep. The journey continues, you are free to follow the road, and peaceful sleep's beauty is waiting for your embrace.

Rest peacefully, let your dreams run wild, and may your evenings be blessed always.

Accept the night because it promises peaceful dreams.

Made in the USA
Middletown, DE
16 November 2023

42870367R00066